THE
FRED FACTOR

How passion in your work and life can
turn the ordinary into the extraordinary

MARK SANBORN

BUSINESS
BOOKS

Published by Random House Business Books in 2004

11

Copyright © 2004 by Mark Sanborn

First published in the United States by Currency Doubleday, a division of
Random House Inc. in 2004

First published in Great Britain in 2004 by
Random House Business Books
The Random House Group Limited
20 Vauxhall Bridge Road, London, SW1V 2SA

www.randomhouse.co.uk

The Random House Group Limited Reg. No. 954009

A CIP catalogue record for this book
is available from the British Library

Addresses for companies within The Random House Group
Limited can be found at: www.randomhouse.co.uk/offices.htm

The Random House Group Limited supports The Forest
Stewardship Council (FSC), the leading international forest
certification organisation. All our titles that are printed on
Greenpeace approved FSC certified paper carry the FSC logo.
Our paper procurement policy can be found at
www.randomhouse.co.uk/environment.

ISBN 9781844138166

Printed in the UK by CPI Bookmarque, Croydon, CR0 4TD

Contents

FOREWORD

Now and then you discover a book that's so inspiring you find yourself immediately making a list of people you know who *must* have a copy!

That was my response upon reading *The Fred Factor* by Mark Sanborn.

This small, engaging book, based on a true story, delivers a potent motivational message that will super-charge your attitude toward work and life. Let's face it—if a guy named Fred, who has a less-than-glamorous job working for the U.S. Postal Service, can serve his customers with exceptional service and commitment, what opportunities await you and me to help others, and in the process achieve deeper personal satisfaction?

If I were to write out a list of individuals who would benefit from reading *The Fred Factor,* here's whom I would include:

- My employees and business associates—for they will learn the secret behind how to better serve customers.
- Professional acquaintances in management positions—for they will be shown how to inspire an entire organization to seek unprecedented levels of excellence.
- My family members—for they will discover the benefit of showing genuine appreciation to those they love.
- Graduating students—for they will find extraordinary

insights into achieving lifelong success not taught in class-rooms.

- Finally, I would wish to place the book in the hands of everyone I know who wants to turn the mundane moments of life into extraordinary experiences.

There are four basic principles that define the "Fred Factor." I won't spoil your excitement of discovery by sharing what they are here. But I promise that if you take Mark Sanborn's advice to heart and begin living a more "Fred-like" existence, you will never view yourself, your value to others, and your importance in the world in the same way again. And not only will you affect your *own* sphere of influence for good, but you will gain the skills to help *others* become "Freds" as well.

Perhaps what I like best about *The Fred Factor* is that this is not just another parable about how to make life work better—as valuable as those fictional stories can be. What makes this book special is that Fred's story is *true!* And in addition to Fred's own story, the book introduces us to many other real people making a difference in the world, in environments as diverse as a doctor's office, a restaurant, a classroom, and a home.

I urge you to do something special for others and *yourself*—incorporate the "Fred Factor" into your life.

—JOHN C. MAXWELL

ACKNOWLEDGMENTS

The real Fred the Postman—Fred Shea—continues to be an inspiration to me. I thank him for being the example of extraordinary service that he is and for allowing me to share his story.

The team at WaterBrook Press I count as friends. Thanks to Don Pape for believing in this book and to Bruce Nygren for his able assistance in editing.

So many friends in the National Speakers Association have inspired, instructed, and encouraged me over the years. Being a member of this fine organization has added tremendously to my personal life as well as my professional life. There are too many speaker-pals to mention by name, but you know who you are. Please also know that I am grateful.

My wife, Darla, has been my biggest fan and encourager. She has proofread many manuscripts, listened to countless speeches, and supported my unusual road-warrior lifestyle. She has, as always, my undying love and gratitude.

And, finally, to the many individuals—some whom I've met and others whom I've only heard about—who live the spirit of the Fred Factor every day and make life fuller and richer for others—I tip my hat to all of you.

To my sons, Hunter and Jack—I'm proud to be your dad.
To my wife, Darla—I'm blessed to be your husband.

PART 1

WHAT'S A FRED?

One

THE FIRST FRED

Make each day your masterpiece.

—JOSHUA WOODEN, father of John Wooden

I first met a "Fred" just after purchasing what I called a "new" old house. Built in 1928, the house was the first I'd owned and was located in a beautiful tree-lined area of Denver called Washington Park. Just days after I moved in, I heard a knock on my front door. When I opened it I saw a mailman standing on my porch.

"Good morning, Mr. Sanborn!" he said cheerfully. "My name is Fred, and I'm your postal carrier. I just stopped by to introduce myself—to welcome you to the neighborhood and find out a little bit about you and what you do for a living."

Fred was an ordinary-looking fellow of average height and build with a small mustache. While his physical appearance didn't convey anything out of the ordinary, his sincerity and warmth were noticeable immediately.

I was a bit startled. Like most of us, I had been receiving mail for years, but I had never had this kind of personal encounter with my postal carrier. I was impressed—nice touch.

"I'm a professional speaker. I don't have a real job," I replied jokingly.

"If you're a professional speaker, you must travel a lot," said Fred.

"Yes, I do. I travel anywhere from 160 to 200 days a year."

Nodding, Fred went on. "Well, if you'll just give me a copy of your schedule, I'll hold your mail and bundle it. I'll only deliver it on the days that you are at home to receive it."

I was amazed by Fred's conscientious offer, but I told him that such extra effort probably wasn't necessary. "Why don't you just leave the mail in the box on the side of the house?" I suggested. "I'll pick it up when I come back into town."

Fred frowned and shook his head. "Mr. Sanborn, burglars often watch for mail building up in a box. That tells them you're out of town. You might become the victim of a break-in." Fred was more worried about my mail than I was! But it made sense; he was the postal professional.

"Here's what I suggest, Mr. Sanborn," Fred continued. "I'll put mail in your box as long as I can get it to close. That way nobody will know you're gone. Whatever doesn't fit in the box, I'll put between the screen door and the front door. Nobody will see it there. And if that area becomes too full of mail, I'll just hold the rest of it for you until you come back into town."

At this point I started to wonder: Does this guy really work for the U.S. Postal Service? Maybe this neighborhood had its own private mail-delivery system. Still, because Fred's suggestions sounded like a terrific plan, I agreed to them.

Two weeks later I returned home from a trip. As I put the key in my-front door lock, I noticed my doormat was missing. Were thieves actually stealing doormats in Denver? Then I saw the mat in a corner of the porch, concealing something. I lifted the mat and found a note from—who else?—Fred! Reading his message, I learned what had happened. While I was gone, a different delivery service had misdelivered a package sent to me. The box had been left on somebody else's porch, five doors down the street. Noticing my box on the wrong porch, Fred had picked it up, carried it to my house, attached his note, and then tried to make the package less noticeable by placing it under the doormat.

Not only was Fred delivering the mail, he was now picking up the slack for UPS!

His actions made a huge impression on me. As a professional speaker, I am particularly adept at finding and pointing out what's "wrong" with customer service and business in general. Finding examples of what's "right" or even praiseworthy is much harder. Yet here was my postman, Fred, a gold-plated example of what personalized service looks like and a role model for anyone who wants to make a difference in his or her work.

I started using my experiences with Fred as illustrations in speeches and seminars that I presented across the United States. Everyone wanted to hear about Fred. Listeners in my audiences were enthralled, whether they worked in the service industry, at a manufacturing company, in high-tech, or in health care.

Back home in Denver, I occasionally had a chance to share with Fred how his work was inspiring others. I told him one story about a discouraged employee who received no recognition from her employers. She wrote to tell me that Fred's example had inspired her to "keep on keeping on" and continue doing what she knew in her heart was the right thing to do, regardless of recognition or reward.

I related to Fred the confession of a manager who had pulled me aside after one speech to tell me he never realized that his career goal all along was to be "a Fred." He believed that excellence and quality should be the goals of every person in any business or profession.

I was delighted to tell my postman that several companies had created a Fred Award to present to employees who demonstrated his trademark spirit of service, innovation, and commitment.

And one fan of Fred once sent him a box of homemade cookies in care of my address!

On the first Christmas after Fred became my postman, I wanted to thank him more formally for his exceptional service. I left a small gift in the mailbox for him. The next day I found an unusual letter in my box. The envelope had a stamp on it, but it wasn't canceled. That's when I noticed the return address; the letter was from Fred the Postman.

Fred knew it would be illegal to put an unpostmarked letter

in the box, so even though he personally carried it from his house to my house, he had done the right thing by placing a stamp on the letter.

I opened the letter, which said in part, "Dear Mr. Sanborn, Thank you for remembering me at Christmas. I am flattered you talk about me in your speeches and seminars, and I hope I can continue to provide exceptional service. Sincerely, Fred the Postman."

Over the next ten years, I received consistently remarkable service from Fred. I could always tell which days he wasn't working my street by the way the mail was jammed into my box. When Fred was on the job, all items were neatly bundled.

But there was more. Fred also took a personal interest in me. One day while I was mowing the front lawn, a vehicle slowed in the street. The window went down and a familiar voice yelled, "Hello, Mr. Sanborn! How was your trip?"

It was Fred, *off duty*, driving around the neighborhood.

After observing his exemplary attitude and actions, I concluded that Fred—and the way he did his job—provides a perfect metaphor for high individual achievement and excellence in the twenty-first century. Fred—and the countless other Freds I've met, observed, or been served by in numerous professions—inspired me to write *The Fred Factor*. It contains the simple yet profound lessons all the Freds around the world have taught me.

Anyone can be a Fred! That includes you! The result will not just be extraordinary effort and success in your work. You'll find yourself living an extraordinary life as well.

Two

THE FRED PRINCIPLES

Whatever you are, be a good one.

—ABRAHAM LINCOLN

Truth is transferable. That's why I will often refer in this book to some core ideas that I believe define the essence of the Fred Factor. These ideas apply to your life and your work. Here, in summary form, are the four principles I learned from Fred the Postman that I believe apply to any person, in any profession, in any situation, at any time.

PRINCIPLE 1: EVERYONE MAKES A DIFFERENCE

It doesn't matter how large or even how ineffective an organization is. An individual can still make a difference. *You* can make a difference. A mediocre employer can hinder exceptional performance, choose to ignore it, and not adequately recognize or encourage it. Or an excellent employer can train employees to achieve exceptional performance and then reward it. Ultimately, though, only the employee can choose to do his or her job in an extraordinary way, regardless of the circumstances.

Think about it. Do you add to or take away from the experience of your customers and colleagues? Do you move your organization closer to or further from its goals? Do you perform your work in an ordinary way, or do you execute it superbly? Do you lighten someone's burden or add to it? Do you lift someone up or put someone down?

Nobody can prevent you from choosing to be exceptional. At the end of the day, the only question that matters is, What kind of difference did you make?

Fred Smith, the distinguished author and business leader, has noted from his years of leadership experience that "most people have a passion for significance."

I agree. Consider Fred the Postman's example. Where others might have seen delivering mail as monotonous drudgery, Fred saw an opportunity to make the lives of his customers more enjoyable. He chose to make a positive difference.

Martin Luther King Jr. said, "If a man is called to be a street sweeper, he should sweep streets even as Michelangelo painted or Beethoven composed music or Shakespeare wrote poetry. He should sweep streets so well that all the hosts of heaven and earth will pause to say, 'Here lived a great street sweeper who did his job well.'"

Fred the Postman understood this. He is proof that there are no insignificant or ordinary jobs when they're performed by significant and extraordinary people.

Politicians are fond of telling us that work gives people dignity. I agree. Having work to do and the means to make a living for oneself and one's family is important. But that is only half the equation. What we haven't been told nearly enough is that *people give work dignity. There are no unimportant jobs, just people who feel unimportant doing their jobs.* That's probably why B. C. Forbes, the legendary founder of *Forbes* magazine, said, "There is more credit and satisfaction in being a first-rate truck driver than a tenth-rate executive."

I have met cab drivers who are more inspired about how they perform their work than some upper-level managers who seem to have lost any drive for excellence. While position never determines performance, ultimately performance determines position in life. That's because position is based on results rather than intentions. It's about actually doing what others usually only talk about.

Setting a higher standard is more challenging than simply achieving the status quo. Withstanding the criticism of those who are threatened by your achievement depends not on your title, but on your attitude. Ultimately, the more valuable you are to others—the more value you create in your work or your interactions with others—the more value will eventually flow toward you. Faithfully doing your best, independent of the support, acknowledgment, or reward of others, is a key determinant in a fulfilling career.

Principle 2: Success Is Built on Relationships

Throughout my life, most of the mail sent to me has ended up in my mailbox. This service was performed by the U.S. Postal Service, which gave me what my postage paid for—nothing more, nothing less.

In contrast, the service I received from Fred the Postman was superior for many reasons, the biggest reason being my relationship with him. It differed from the relationship I've had with any other postal carrier, before or since. In fact, Fred is the only postal carrier I've ever had a personal relationship with.

It's easy to see why Fred stood above the crowd. Indifferent people deliver impersonal service. Service becomes personalized when a relationship exists between the provider and the customer. Fred took time to get to know me and to understand my needs and preferences. He then used that information to provide better service than I had ever received before. Do you have this capability?

Fred is proof that in any job or business, relationship building is the most important objective because the quality of the relationship determines the quality of the product or service. That's also why

- leaders succeed when they recognize that their employees are human;
- technology succeeds when it recognizes that its users are human; and
- employees like Fred the Postman succeed when they recognize their work involves interacting with human beings.

Principle 3: You Must Continually Create Value for Others, and It Doesn't Have to Cost a Penny

Do you ever complain that you don't have enough money? the necessary training? the right opportunities? In other words, do you believe that you lack resources to perform at a higher level?

Then consider Fred. What resources did he have at his disposal? A drab blue uniform and a bag full of mail. That's it! Yet he walked up and down streets with his heart and head stirred by possibilities. His imagination enabled him to create value for his customers, and he didn't need an extra dollar to do it. He just thought harder and more creatively than other postal carriers.

In doing this Fred mastered the most important job skill of the twenty-first century: the ability to create value for customers without spending more money to do it.

You, too, can replace money with imagination. The object is to outthink your competition rather than outspend them.

I've met many people who were concerned that they might become victims of downsizing and lose their jobs. I always tell them to quit worrying. My indifference shocks them. Actually my intent is to refocus their attention from being employed to being "employable."

In today's economy, a high-school or college graduate should expect to be unemployed a few times during his or her career. But that unemployment will be brief as long as the individual is employable. Being employable means having a skill set that makes you desirable to any employer, regardless of industry or geographic location.

So what does that skill set look like? Many factors contribute to employability, but I am convinced that the most critical skill is the ability to create value for customers and colleagues without spending money to do it. The trick is to replace money with imagination, to substitute creativity for capital.

Sanborn's Maxim says that the faster you try to solve a problem with money, the less likely it will be the best solution. With enough money anyone can buy his or her way out of a problem. The challenge is to outthink rather than to outspend the competition.

In the world of business, the competition is either inside or outside the organization, and sometimes both. For example, you may be competing for a better position in your department or company. While professional decorum might prevent you from describing it this way, you hope that the best man or woman for the job will get it, and you're working to prove you're that person.

Or there may be an identified competitor in the marketplace.

Once, when I spoke at a conference cosponsored by a delivery service that considers the U.S. Postal Service a competitor, I was forbidden to use the story of Fred in my presentation. (It struck me as odd that the company wouldn't want me to use Fred as an example of the kind of service it aspired to and encouraged all of its employees to deliver. But that's the topic of another book!) Because Fred's employer competes for revenue against alternative carriers, Fred either helps or hinders the cause of his company. Most employers recognize that Fred is the kind of employee who will give them a competitive advantage.

But I'm not sure Fred (or his employer) really thought about competition in the traditional sense. Fred is more likely living proof that there is another less observable competitor: *the job we could have done.* The truth is that we compete against our own potential every day. And most of us fall short of what we are capable of doing or being.

I may never understand all that motivates Fred, but I suspect the gratification he gets from excelling in his work and service is a big factor, as is the joy he consistently creates in his customers.

At the end of each day, Fred has beaten a silent opponent that threatens his potential, just as it threatens yours and mine. That competitor is mediocrity, a willingness to do just enough and nothing more to get by.

And while this competitor may not beat you out for a job promotion or take away corporate market share, mediocrity will just as surely diminish the quality of your performance and the meaning you derive from it.

PRINCIPLE 4: YOU CAN REINVENT YOURSELF REGULARLY

Here's something to consider: If Fred could bring such originality to putting mail in a box, how much more could you and I do to bring originality to what we do? How can we reinvent ourselves and our work?

There are days when you wake up tired. You figure you've read the books, listened to the audiotapes, watched the videos, and sat through the training sessions. You're doing everything you can possibly do to produce personal excellence, but you're still fatigued and unmotivated. When your life is at low tide, when your professional commitment is wavering and you just want to get the job done and go home at the end of the day, what can you do?

Here's what I do: I think about the guy who used to deliver my mail. Because if Fred the Postman could bring that kind of creativity and commitment to putting mail in a box, I can do as much or more to reinvent my work and rejuvenate my efforts. I believe that no matter what job you hold, what industry you work in, or where you live, every morning you wake up with a clean slate. You can make your business, as well as your life, anything you choose it to be.

That's what I call the Fred Factor.

Three

FRED SIGHTINGS

There comes a special moment in everyone's life,
a moment for which that person was born. That
special opportunity, when he seizes it, will fulfill his
mission—a mission for which he is uniquely qual-
ified. In that moment, he finds greatness. It is his
finest hour.

—WINSTON CHURCHILL

Now that I've explained the qualities of a typical Fred, you
will better understand why I enjoy discovering Freds wher-
ever I go.

I love Starbucks coffee and rarely start my day without it.
One morning as I was driving to Denver International Airport, I
swung by Starbucks for my favorite drink, a grande (a really large
cup of steaming coffee).

Back on the interstate I realized that I had created a bit of a
dilemma. My car didn't have an automatic transmission, which
meant I needed one hand to shift and the other to drive. I set my

coffee down on the center console until I could accelerate to a higher gear. What were the odds that the coffee would spill?

Pretty high odds, actually. Suddenly, a dark, hot stain spread over my right leg, from my knee to my hip. And I was wearing *light blue* jeans. At the airport I applied some jean first aid by squeegeeing my pants and using the rest-room hand dryer. But I still looked like a giant dork.

As soon as I checked into the Airport Marriott in Atlanta, I called housekeeping. "These coffee-stained jeans are the only pants I have to wear for my return trip home," I explained to the supervisor. "Is there any chance I can get them washed overnight?"

With a lot of sympathy in her voice, she informed me that not only was there no guest laundry, but the crew that washed linens had left for the day. But she said she would be glad to pick up my jeans, take them home, and wash and return them early the next morning.

Thankful for her kindness, I agreed to this plan.

The next morning this incredible woman delivered a clean pair of freshly washed and pressed jeans to my door.

I still regret that I didn't get her name (although I did write a glowing letter about her to the hotel). But even though I don't know her given name, I know what to call her: She's a Fred.

Ever since I met Fred the Postman, I've come to realize that Freds—as well as potential Freds—are everywhere. And every one I meet convinces me that Freds are a lot less the exception to the rule than I once thought. Each one is truly an individual in his or her own way. Here are some Fred types I've encountered.

A FUNNY FRED

Passengers on the 6:15 a.m. flight from Denver to San Francisco are rarely at their perkiest. From experience I know the flight is usually uneventful, and all that is heard is an occasional snore. Of course, this can change depending on the flight attendant.

On one flight the passengers were treated to some unorthodox announcements from an unusually creative and witty flight attendant.

"If you are having a hard time getting your ears to pop, I suggest you yawn widely," she began. "And if you are having a hard time yawning, ask me and I'll tell you about my love life."

"We are on final approach into San Francisco airport. If San Francisco is your final destination, I hope you'll have a safe drive home. There is some blockage on the northbound 101, and it appears there is a stalled car at the Market Street exit. But otherwise, traffic appears to be moving smoothly."

By now the usually sleepy passengers were waking up; laughter was heard throughout the airplane. After we touched down, the flight attendant was back for an encore.

"Unless the person next to you has beaten me to it, let me be the first to welcome you to San Francisco. You'll notice that the airport buildings are in the distance. We don't land at the terminal because it scares the heck out of the people inside. That's why we land way out here. That means we'll need to taxi, so please don't stand up until we are parked at the gate and the seat-belt sign has been turned off.

"For those of you who are 1Ks, Premiers, and frequent fliers—there are too many of you on board to mention by name, but you know who you are—we thank you for choosing United for your extensive travels. And if you'll leave me a recent picture as you deplane, I'll be glad to mail it to your loved ones so they remember what you look like.

"My final hope is that when you leave the airplane, you'll do so with a big smile on your face. That way the people outside will wonder just what it is we do up here in the friendly skies."

Here's what this Fred did: She took some risks and had some fun. As a result, the passengers—or rather her "customers"—had fun too.

An Accountable Fred

Jack Foy works as a night auditor at Homewood Suites in Worthington, Ohio. One night, which happened to be Father's Day eve, a woman whose husband was staying at the property called with a special request. She told Jack that for Father's Day the man's daughter wanted to make sure her dad had his favorite breakfast of pancakes, eggs, and bacon.

The only problem was that Homewood Suites doesn't have a

restaurant. So at 7:00 a.m. when Jack got off work, he drove to a nearby restaurant to pick up the special meal. He also bought a card and used a crayon to sign it "From Daddy's Little Girl." Then he drove back to the hotel and delivered the care package to one very astonished and grateful guest.

Oh, and by the way, as a result of Jack's act of service, the man he had taken such good care of gave Jack's hotel a substantial contract. Value-added accounting.

Now that's Fred power!

A Generous Fred

I had just checked into the Crowne Plaza in Columbus, Ohio, when I discovered that I didn't have enough cash to catch a cab back to the airport the next morning. The person at the front desk told me that the hotel couldn't advance me any cash on my American Express card, and unfortunately, I didn't have my ATM card with me. I was informed, however, that some cabs did take credit cards. But since I was scheduled to end my speech at 9:00 a.m. and wanted to catch a 9:40 flight, I was afraid that the additional time required to line up an accommodating cab and fill out the accompanying paperwork would make it even more difficult to make my flight.

My troubles didn't end there. I found that my room key didn't work, so I headed down the hall to the house phone which was located directly outside the clubroom. The man on duty in the bar noticed that I was making a call and that I still had all my luggage.

"Is there a problem?" he inquired, introducing himself as Nick. I explained that my room key wouldn't work.

"I'll take care of it," he said, and then he asked, "Would you like a drink on me for your inconvenience?" I accepted his offer and sipped and ate some snacks while Nick called for a new key to be brought up.

Nick was so helpful that once I had my key, I decided to share my embarrassing dilemma with him. He listened and said, "If all else fails, check back with me and I'll take care of it."

He informed me that he was on duty until 7:30 the next morning and asked, "Shall I call you to make sure you have the money you need before I leave?" I told him that would be very thoughtful.

Finally in my room, I spent the next forty minutes on the phone with my office, my bank, and American Express. Nothing worked. I was having "one of those days." My personal banker said there was nothing she could do. American Express could provide cash, but the process would require D-day–like planning. I decided to go back to Nick.

"This is embarrassing, Nick," I confessed. "I've traveled all over the world and run out of money only twice in twenty years. I hate to ask, but can I borrow twenty dollars from you?"

"No problem! These things happen," Nick replied without a moment's hesitation. Opening his wallet, he said, "Here, take thirty." I tried to explain that I only needed twenty dollars.

"No, no, take the thirty," he insisted. "You never know what might come up." We exchanged addresses, and I promised to send him the money as soon as I arrived home.

I was both gratified and stunned by Nick's generous assistance. A problem that couldn't be expediently solved by American Express, Norwest Bank, or even my own office was worked out by one helpful individual who was willing to be of service.

Thirty dollars isn't a lot of money, but neither is it a minor amount, especially when it comes out of one's pocket. Nick had never seen me before, and for all he knew, he would never see or hear from me again. He understood the risks associated with truly being of service, and still he was willing to accept them.

When I returned to my office the next day, I mailed Nick a check along with some of my books and tapes to express my appreciation.

Has Nick ever been stiffed? Has he ever helped out a guest who failed to either appreciate or repay him? I don't know, but my sense is that he would continue to be of service even if those people he helps don't always repay him.

I believe that about Nick because I believe he knows some important truths about life. He knows that the way to move through life joyfully and successfully is by focusing on what you give rather than on what you get. He knows that you don't do the right thing just because you have to do it. You do it because it is the right thing to do. Nick knows that being of service isn't an obligation, but an opportunity. He knows that being helpful is even more fun than being helped.

It is kind of funny, but I'm actually glad I ran out of money because I got to meet Nick and be reminded of what Nick knows. And because of that, you now know too.

A FAMOUS FRED

Finding a summer job in the Bronx in the early 1950s wasn't easy, but young Colin was determined to earn the money he needed. He showed up early every morning at the Teamsters Hall to volunteer for day jobs. Sometimes he landed a spot on a soda delivery truck as a helper. Then a job cleaning up sticky soda syrup opened up at a Pepsi plant. None of the other kids volunteered, but Colin did. And he did such a good job that he was invited back the following summer. That summer he operated a bottling machine instead of a mop, and by the end of the summer, he was a deputy shift leader.

It taught him an important lesson. "All work is honorable," he wrote in his memoirs. "Always do your best because someone is watching."

Years later the world watched Colin Powell serve as the

chairman of the Joint Chiefs of Staff, lead the military effort in the Gulf War, and establish himself as a champion of education. In 2000 he was chosen as secretary of state by President-elect George W. Bush.

MORE FRED SIGHTINGS

Here are some other candidates for the Fred Hall of Fame:

- A waitress had just finished her shift at Morton's of Chicago. As she was walking to her car, she recognized a man in the parking lot as a guest she had served earlier in the evening. He was struggling, quite unsuccessfully, to change the flat tire on his car. "Let me help," she offered. In short order this enterprising waitress got the tire changed and sent the restaurant patron on his way.

- On a flight to Orlando, the fun-loving steward put on a Goofy cap and invited the children to join him in the front of the cabin where he did magic tricks for them. A flight attendant on the same flight sat on the floor with a child in her lap, giving a frazzled parent a much-needed break from child care.

- At Crested Butte Mountain Ski Resort, an employee repaired a skier's disabled car in the parking lot. After work, another employee used his own forest-service permit to cut down a tree so that a family who was staying at the resort would have a Christmas tree for their holiday vacation.

- A cable installer in Southern California does a lot more than his official job description. He programs the remote switcher for the new channels, sets the timer on the VCR, and often improves sound quality by repositioning the stereo antenna and speakers.

- A friend of mine recently went to the movies and forgot her wallet. When she asked an employee if she could write a check, she was told not to worry about it. Instead, she was instructed to drop the money off the next time she was nearby. After she had taken her seat, the same employee brought her a complimentary box of popcorn and a soft drink. How often does my friend go to that movie theater? Every chance she gets.

- Once I had a particularly unpleasant experience trying to get home to Denver from Philadelphia. The airline personnel I encountered at the airport seemed unable or unwilling to help, so I called the toll-free number for frequent fliers and requested a supervisor. She was genuinely empathic and went to great lengths to make sure I was booked on a flight that night. Her hard work was greatly appreciated, but even more impressive was the fact that she called my office the next day to make sure I had made it home okay!

Freds, indeed, are everywhere. You probably have encountered a few yourself.

The time has come to ask the critical question: Are you ready to be a Fred? If so, then keep reading!

PART 2

BECOMING
A FRED

After reading this far you may be saying, "I wish I knew, lived, and worked with more people like Fred the Postman!" We would all benefit from a world populated by people like Fred—people who take that kind of pride in their work and turn the ordinary into the extraordinary.

How many "Freds" are in your organization? Have you ever found yourself saying, "I wish we had more people like that around here!"? Do you regret that some of your teammates might more accurately be described as "anti-Freds"?

So how can we get more Freds in the world? That's easy to answer: *Be a Fred!*

It can all start with you. If you want a world with more Freds, be a Fred. Only when you make the ordinary extraordinary will others see the possibilities for themselves.

It isn't that hard. Actually, it's harder *not* to be a Fred. The skills and abilities that enable us to be "Fred-like" often come naturally; they come out of who we already are. If you didn't have at least an interest (or, more likely, a burning desire) to make the most of your career and relationships, you wouldn't have made it this far into the book.

One thing seems common to all human beings: a passion for significance. I've never met anyone who wanted to be insignificant. Everyone wants to count, to know that what he or she does each day isn't simply a means of making a living, but "a living of making meaning." The unhappiest people of all may well be those who go to jobs they hate because they need the money. Why not go to a job you *love* because you need the money?

You can. Convert your job into one you love, not by doing a different job, but by doing the one you have differently!

That's what made Fred unique. Thousands of men and women deliver the mail. For some it is "just a job." For many it may be an occupation they enjoy. But for a few like Fred, delivering the mail becomes a calling.

The person doing the work determines the difference between the mundane and the magnificent.

You Choose

Which do you prefer: enjoyment or misery? feeling good about your work or feeling bad about it? being yourself or hiding the real you? It is harder to be miserable, negative, and insincere than it is to be happy, positive, and genuine. All Freds share those latter characteristics, no matter what type of work they do.

Most people think they get ahead in life by learning something new. I believe you can also get ahead by going back to the basics of success. There are lots of ways to define true success, but I believe that having the most fun doing your best work is at the top of the list.

All it takes is reestablishing the things you've always known—

or the lessons you learned in kindergarten or Sunday school—
and starting to reapply them to your life and your work.

Do the Right Thing for the Right Reason

Here's a mystery: If you expect praise and recognition, it will sel-
dom come. I really don't know why, but life has demonstrated
repeatedly that if your motive for doing something is to receive
thanks or praise, you'll often be disappointed. If, however, you go
about doing the right thing, knowing that the doing is its own
reward, you'll be fulfilled whether or not you get recognition from
others. When reward or recognition comes, it will be icing on
the cake.

Your Possibilities Are Endless

Here's my take on why people love to hear the story of Fred the
Postman: It reminds them not only of what is possible but of their
own personal potential as well. Excellence, wisdom, and dedica-
tion are all functioning parts of Fred's world. The mediocrity,
foolishness, and lack of commitment we encounter every day seem
poor substitutes.

Freds remind us that we can choose the right role models.
Freds set an inspiring example for their companies and organizations, teammates, customers, friends, and families. When others

see the infinite ways to create excellence and "wow" in their work, then they, too, will want to become Freds. Something wonderful will happen. The energy they once had will be restored. Enthusiasm will replace cynicism, and action will overcome complacency. The feedback, recognition, and satisfaction that come from being a Fred will fuel ongoing, quality efforts.

Four

EVERYONE MAKES
A DIFFERENCE

All men matter. You matter. I matter. It's the hardest
thing in theology to believe.

—G. K. CHESTERTON

It was a beautiful spring morning in Cincinnati. Since I wasn't
scheduled to speak until the afternoon, I left my hotel and
found a nearby coffee shop. After paying for a cup (free refills!),
I strolled outside to sit at a sidewalk table and read my newspaper.
For the next twenty minutes, I enjoyed the reading and sipping.

A cabstand was nearby, and I noticed an older woman at the
wheel of the second cab in line. She got out to stretch and looked
at the coffee shop behind me. I didn't need to be clairvoyant to
realize she was thinking about going inside. I got up and walked
over to her. "Care for a cup of coffee?" I asked.

"That'd be great!" she replied.

"How do you take it?"

"Black." She was my kind of coffee drinker.

I went into the coffee shop, got my free refill, and paid a little over a dollar for the cabbie's coffee. When I returned to the cabbie, she was digging in her pockets for change.

"Don't worry about it," I said. "The coffee's on me."

As I picked up my paper and started back to the hotel, the last thing I saw was the woman standing speechless, a look of amazement on her face.

That buck and change was the best money I spent that day. I was a Fred, which gave me a whole lot of satisfaction. And maybe I passed on some inspiration, too.

DID YOU WAKE UP THIS MORNING INTENDING TO CHANGE THE WORLD?

To admit that you begin the day planning to change the world certainly sounds grandiose, maybe even delusional. Yet I believe that you do change the world every day, whether you intend to or not. Often it only takes a small act to make a big difference.

You change the world of your spouse or kids, depending on how you interact with them before you leave the house. A little extra time and attention or a tender moment of affection changes their world that day. And it reminds you of what is important when the mad dash to the office irks you and makes you feel that the day is off to a rough start.

You change the world of another driver when you allow her to change lanes abruptly without blaring your horn, recognizing that she, too, is human and fallible. Of course, you alter her world in a different way if you blast your horn, yell, and gesture obscenely.

You also change the world of a coworker, a customer, a vendor, or a cafeteria worker with your smile or your frown.

No, these aren't dramatic changes. They won't alter the course of world affairs or bring about a cure for AIDS. But who's to say that these little changes don't have a cumulative, profound effect in the lives of others and, ultimately, in your *own* life?

Everybody Makes a Difference Every Day

You can read books on how to make a difference. You have probably heard teachers, pastors, and speakers exhorting their listeners to "make a difference."

The fact is that everybody is already making a difference every day. The key question is, What *kind* of difference is each of us making?

To make a difference means affecting another person, group, or situation. It is nearly impossible to remain neutral as you journey through each day. Paying attention to others, giving them the respect they deserve, and politely serving them makes a positive difference.

In contrast, neglecting, criticizing, and belittling others, whether intentionally or not, produces a negative difference.

The key is to pay attention to the kinds of differences you are making. As my friend and motorcycle-riding buddy Jim Cathcart says, "To know more, notice more."

You shouldn't be asking, "Did I make a difference today?" Of course you did! You undoubtedly affected somebody, maybe slightly, maybe significantly.

The most important question to ask yourself is, What *kind* of difference did I make?

Even Better Than Random Acts of Kindness

Maybe you've seen the bumper sticker "Practice Random Acts of Kindness." That's good advice, but I have something to add: Why not "Practice Acts of the Extraordinary Regularly"?

Even the least Fred-like person can occasionally—even "accidentally"—do something outstanding. When it happens, we should recognize and celebrate it by positively reinforcing the behavior.

The purpose of this book is to help you think, act, and become Fred-like, to bring the same spirit of magnanimity to your work, relationships, and life as Fred did to his—not periodically, but persistently. You can learn to look at the world through "Fred-colored glasses."

The things you do, both small and large, cumulatively create a lifestyle that becomes apparent to anybody paying the slightest attention. It's that kind of example that most influences others.

The Power of a Committed Individual

It's helpful to be reminded of how far-reaching our impact on others can be.

In 1962 Dick Jordan was a rookie teacher at George Washington High School in Denver. He invited students to meet him on the first day of the millennium at the west entrance of the Denver Public Library downtown. On the appointed day, nearly thirty years later, some three hundred students showed up.

When reporters asked them why they had come, the answers were simple: They felt that Jordan cared for them. He taught them how to think and to question what was in history books, and in at least one case, he had inspired a student to become a teacher. The husband of one student came because it was one of the last things his wife had asked of him as she was dying of cancer.

It had begun as a kind of joke. As a poor college graduate, Jordan had to borrow three hundred dollars from a Denver public schools recruiter just to make the trip to Colorado. He wore the same brown suit to school for three years.

He told his very first class, "I can retire in the year 2000. We ought to meet somewhere on that New Year's Day. And everybody bring a dollar because I'm going to need it!"

His students remembered. The dollars they brought were donated to the Catholic Worker Soup Kitchen.

The Difference of a Great Idea

Bonnie McClurg understands how to make a difference. As a reading teacher at Chandler Elementary School in Charleston, West Virginia, Bonnie changes lives.

Nine years ago she observed that students bought snacks from the school vending machine every day. This prompted her to think and take a leap forward: Why not make books as easy and inexpensive to buy as snack food? Quickly moving on her idea, she found a way to stock books alongside the pretzels and corn chips inside that vending machine.

Since then, students have been able to purchase books like *The Velveteen Rabbit* and *Amazing World of Dinosaurs* for just fifty cents each, marked down from as much as $7.95. Is it any surprise that more than one thousand books have been purchased by eager students? Bonnie didn't sit on her idea; she made it happen. And she showed students that books can be enjoyable "snacks" too, ones that are always good for them.

Three Difference-Making Strategies

There are good ways and not so good ways to go about influencing your world. Here are some proven standards for doing it right.

Strategy 1: Identify when you'll make a difference. When can you make a difference? At every opportunity! Remember, nobody is forcing you to do extraordinary things. If your attempts at being a Fred become an oppressive duty, you're bound to fail. You're making a difference because, like most of the Freds I've encountered, you want to and you can.

Strategy 2: Target the people to whom you'll make a difference. Fred the Postman seems intent on providing exceptional service to all his customers. Is that possible for you and me? The answer is "It depends." I believe that doing a great job for everyone you serve, at home or in business, is possible. Undoubtedly there are those people, however, whom you want to do something *extraordinary* for. The most important people in our lives deserve our best attention:

- *Customers.* It would have been easy to write a book on customer service and use Fred the Postman as the primary illustration, but I wanted what I've learned from Fred and others like him to go beyond the marketplace and into every area of human relationships. I do acknowledge, however, that perhaps the easiest application and the quickest payoff are to begin by serving your customers as Fred served me. You'll instantly earn their attention and, soon, their unwavering devotion.

- *Family.* How would your spouse react if you demonstrated Fred-like care and commitment to him or her? What about your kids? One of the sadder things in life is to know someone loves us but to rarely experience it. You can transform ordinary family interactions and events into extraordinary moments and experiences by applying these principles at home.

- *Boss.* Would you like to work for an incredible boss? Then start by treating your boss like an incredible person. Do extraordinary things for him or her, and over time I bet you'll notice a difference in your relationship. And if you don't, it's time to look for a new boss.

- *Teammates.* High-performance teams are made up of high-performance teammates. Somebody has to go first; why not you? Become the Fred of your team or depart-ment and watch as others are positively affected.

- *Friends and strangers.* What are you doing to enrich the lives of those you know and those you don't? The only thing more fantastic than experiencing an "Act of Fred" from someone you know is experiencing it from a com-plete stranger. It restores one's faith in the potential of human behavior.

Strategy 3: Be the difference. A little thought and reflection will quickly help you see the difference you can make in any activity or event. Often our lives are so busy and stressful that we don't have time to consider the differences that would enrich and add value to whatever we do for others. This means that we must make time in our schedules to determine how we can change our ordinary actions into extraordinary ones. Just as athletes prepare for competition in pregame meetings, we, too, should prepare for our daily activities with pregame thought.

Once we know the difference we can make, our challenge is to be the difference maker. True difference making can't be delegated. It's up to us to take action.

What kind of difference will you make today?

Five

SUCCESS IS BUILT ON RELATIONSHIPS

You add value to people when you value them.

—JOHN C. MAXWELL

One evening before making my presentation at a sales conference, I discovered that the vice president of sales for a large food products firm and I were both big "motor-heads" (car lovers).

"Do you read *AutoWeek*?" he asked.

At the time I wasn't familiar with the publication, but after he told me about the magazine and what it covered, I made a mental note to subscribe to it.

My fellow motor-head was one step ahead of me. The next morning before my speech, he handed me a subscription card that he had pulled out of his most recent issue.

I was struck by how thoughtful this small gesture was. As a result I use a similar technique when I talk with friends and clients about books. If I find out that there is a really great title they've not read, I'll order a copy and have it sent to them with my compliments. That way we both get a lot of satisfaction, and we also fortify our bond with each other and extend the range of our conversations.

That's quite a payoff for a simple act of relationship building!

Success Is Built One Relationship at a Time

Every day we interact with dozens of people. Often those interactions are fleeting and unmemorable. Freds, however, don't use people as a means to an end; they use relationships to build a foundation for success. They understand that all outcomes are created by and through interactions with others. So they become students of social psychology. They understand that strong relationships create loyalty and are the basis of partnerships and teamwork.

The best Freds build networks to develop distribution channels for their talents, and they strive to work well with others, whether one-on-one with a customer or in a team with colleagues.

Remember that the quality of a relationship is related directly to the amount of time invested in it. Make sure you give some of your best time to your relationships.

FREDS BUILD RELATIONSHIPS—EVEN WITH
THREE-YEAR-OLDS

HMOs and PPOs have prescribed limits on the amount and types of services they allow health-care providers to give. Despite these limitations, there are still extraordinary health-care workers who focus on what they can do instead of what they can't. With all the complaining about health care, you might not expect to find a stellar example of a Fred in this field.

Yet Dan, a physician's assistant at a pediatrician's office, is a Fred. Imagine working day after day with sick kids!

One day my wife, Darla, took our three-year-old son, Hunter, in for an examination. We wanted to be sure that a fall on the grandparents' coffee table hadn't broken his nose. Hunter was sitting on the floor when Dan came in. After a cheerful greeting, Dan plopped down on the floor next to him.

Hunter watched suspiciously while snacking on pretzels. "Hey, dude, can I have one?" asked Dan. Like most children, Hunter had become a bit leery of what he sometimes has to experience during examinations at the doctor's office. So it wasn't surprising when Hunter's eyes got a little bigger as Dan brazenly reached out and took a pretzel from the bag.

Suddenly a big smile broke across my son's face. Dan proceeded to "interact" in medical terms—in normal language, he and Hunter played. They wrestled and goofed around, and Dan tied

Hunter's shoelaces together. When Hunter saw this, he tried to walk and, predictably, he tripped. He loved it and laughed with glee.

After several minutes of frivolity, Dan was able to examine a totally stress-free little boy. Hunter probably thought he'd misjudged the situation and wasn't really in a medical facility after all.

Dan knew what to do. Not only did he perform his examination with a minimum of fuss, but he actually eliminated the fears of a three-year-old.

Now that's Fred-like relationship building at its best!

The Seven Bs of Relationship Building

In today's technology-driven world, relationship building might be considered a lost art form. Most of us have never been taught how to go about building relationships with others. Whatever we've learned, we've picked up through observation of role models rather than from conscious learning.

We were lucky if we had good role models when we were growing up and not so lucky if we didn't.

Do you want to improve your relationships at home and at work? The following principles will definitely help.

1. Be real. Aside from Fred's extraordinary customer focus, what was most inspiring about him was his uniqueness. He was who he was. I never got the sense Fred was trying to impress me by being anybody but himself.

This is the direct opposite of the prevailing wisdom in our culture today, which is "fake it until you make it." The intent is to become who you want to be by acting as if you are already that person. The only problem with that strategy is that you're a fake!

Try this alternative: Always do your best at being yourself. Sure, you should aim to improve, try new things, and add value. But let these actions come out of who you really are, what you truly believe in, and the things you are committed to.

The prerequisite for relationship building is trust. At its most basic level, trust is built on believing that people are who they represent themselves to be.

2. Be interested (not just interesting). It may be true that interesting people attract attention, but I believe that *interested* people attract appreciation.

When I first met Fred, he quickly introduced himself, but the focus was on how he could best help me meet my needs. I instantly liked Fred because he showed a genuine interest in me, not because he was interesting (although I've learned over time that he certainly is). If Fred had spent time telling me what a great mailman he was, the outcome would have been different.

People are flattered when you express an interest in getting to know them better, not out of morbid curiosity, but in an effort to help or serve them more effectively. Appreciating the people we serve, I believe, increases the value of our service to them.

3. Be a better listener. When you take an interest in and listen to people, they provide important practical information you can use to create value. For instance, listen carefully to your boss, and you might learn that he or she hates to read long memos. You now know that you can improve your working relationship by providing a brief summary. Or at lunch ask a client about her family. You may learn that her fourteen-year-old son has a hobby that one of your children enjoys. Offering to exchange information about that shared interest will add both value and depth to this relationship.

People are flattered when you make an effort to get to know them and seek information on how to serve them better. Understanding and appreciating what they want increases the value of what you can provide for them.

4. Be empathic. If you're interested in others and make the effort to truly know them by listening to them, you'll better understand how they feel. This is empathy. The need to be understood is one of the highest human needs, but too often people who know us either don't care or don't make the effort to understand how we really feel.

Two thousand years ago a wise man named Philo Judaeus said, "Be kind. Everyone you meet is fighting a tough battle." Not much has changed since. His counsel is the essence of practical empathy.

5. Be honest. I summarize all business strategy with this simple idea: Say what you'll do, and do what you say. In other words, don't make promises you can't keep. Don't create expectations you can't fulfill. Avoid overrepresenting and overpromising. Be a man, woman, or organization of your word. That's integrity.

6. Be helpful. Little things make a big difference. Lots of small things cumulatively make a huge difference.

Years ago my friend Ken taught me a neat way to be of service to strangers. If I see one person in a group taking a picture of all the others, I offer to snap the picture so everybody can be included.

Even holding a door open is an indication of Fred-like behavior. So remember your manners, and people will remember you.

7. Be prompt. Time is the one thing many people have far less of than money. Helping them save time by being prompt and efficient is a gift of great value.

BEYOND INTERACTIONS

Here's a test: What percentage of your interactions with others is transactional as opposed to relational?

Transactional interactions focus primarily on results, sometimes even at the cost of relationships. People who value results over relationships are often called "direct." That means they go directly for the outcome, making others feel devalued and even used.

Relational interactions emphasize the importance of how

people are treated in the process of achieving results. This type of interaction doesn't ignore the outcome, but it does recognize that the means are an important part of the end. Fred the Postman was living proof that how you deliver the mail affects how people feel about the outcome.

Not every interaction needs to be relational. Sometimes a lack of time or the situation just doesn't allow it. For example, in an emergency or crisis, getting people to safely evacuate a burning building may require harsh, direct instructions.

Jimmy Buffett once said (and I paraphrase): It takes just about the same amount of time to be a nice guy as it does to be a jerk.

More often than not, you and I can be more Fred-like by taking time to focus on the relational aspect of our interactions. It doesn't take much extra time or effort to be interested and demonstrate the value we have for others, especially those on whom we depend for mutual success.

And that is the essence of building relationships, whether business or personal.

Six

CONTINUALLY CREATE
VALUE FOR OTHERS

> There are two types of people who never achieve very
> much in their lifetimes. One is the person who won't
> do what he or she is told to do, and the other is the
> person who does no more than he or she is told to do.
>
> —ANDREW CARNEGIE

During the Middle Ages it was believed that an alchemist (a person who practiced chemistry, philosophy, and magic) had the ability to turn basic metals into gold. Science has since proven that it's impossible to turn iron into gold. But what most people haven't discovered is that it is possible to turn the most ordinary ideas into ones of great value.

Fred the Postman is a present-day alchemist, and you can learn how to be one too.

A restaurateur was once asked the secret of his success. He said he had benefited from working in the kitchen of a great

European restaurant. There he had learned that the key to greatness was to make everything as good as it could be, regardless of whether it was a complicated entrée or a simple side dish.

"If you serve french fries," he said, "make sure they're the best french fries in the world."

Freds either create new value or add value to the work they do. At the same time, they know that something done—whether for a customer or a colleague—that doesn't provide value could be a waste of both time and energy.

Freds compete successfully by offering better ideas, products, and services than their competitors. They do more than talk about "value-added"; they deliver on it.

The best Freds are true artists at taking ordinary products or job responsibilities and services and making them extraordinary. They are real-world alchemists who practice the art and science of "value creation."

Freds create extra value by doing more than is necessary and exceeding our expectations—most of the time for no extra pay.

I once worked with a hospital that was committed to improving patient relations. One little idea made a big difference: Whenever patients or visitors asked for directions, rather than simply telling them how to get where they wanted to go, the staff member personally escorted them, especially in cases where people were confused or perplexed.

Anyone who has to go to a hospital, whether as a patient or a visitor, is bound to be somewhat bewildered. Having a personal escort relieves people of extra stress they don't need. The hospital staff provided extra value by relieving a burden.

A Crash Course in Adding Value

This is a small book with a big mission: to help you make your life meaningful beyond anything you could have imagined! The following pages include some of the more important ideas I'll share. Are you ready to learn how to be a person of incredible value to others? Here's how that occurs:

1. Tell the truth. Truth seems to be in increasingly short supply. In the marketplace we've become used to being told what others think we want to hear instead of what's really happening. An inquiry into delivery time gets a commitment for "first thing in the morning." By the end of the following day the package still hasn't arrived.

Truth telling should be a basic rather than a value-added opportunity. A philosopher once commented that if honesty did not exist, someone would invent it as the best way of getting rich. Ironically, truth is often so scarce today that we assign an even higher value to it than we did in the past.

2. Practice personality power. I had just finished dining on the patio of one of my favorite Italian restaurants in Denver. My server was nice, but not exceptional. I had observed an older gentleman who was filling water glasses and chatting with patrons. As I was paying my check, he approached to see if I needed a refill. His enthusiasm was genuine as he put his hand lightly on my shoulder and said, "We're glad you came in today."

Those brief words brought an extraordinary conclusion to an otherwise unexceptional dining experience. What I had felt firsthand was the power of personality, what happens when we extend ourselves to others genuinely and enthusiastically. This gentleman had turned filling water glasses and chatting into a fine art by injecting his own personality into the process.

3. Attract through artistry. What are you doing to add an artistic flourish to your products or services? It can be as simple as a unique signature or as significant as a major improvement in packaging or design. We are drawn to attractiveness not only in people but in goods, services, architecture, and all avenues of design.

Freds pay attention to appearances, not because appearances are more important than substance, but because they count. Something of great value unpleasantly presented loses value. Conversely, we increase the value of things when we make them aesthetically pleasing.

4. Meet needs in advance. This is the power of anticipation. Have you ever rented a car, received directions to your destination, and then promptly become lost? Wouldn't it be a nice gesture at the rental counter if someone with a Fred-like mentality wrote down his or her direct-dial number so you could call from your cell phone if you got lost?

If you know that your next-door neighbors are going on vacation next week, why not offer to pick up their mail or water their plants while they're gone? Often people forget about the details that need to be taken care of until the very last minute. Anticipating how you can be of service while your neighbors are gone is a magnanimous gesture that will create great value.

5. *Add "good stuff."* Think of your current position. Is there anything you could add to your teammates' or customers' experiences that would make their lives more enjoyable?

Here are a few things guaranteed to add value regardless of your product, service, or work:

- *Enjoyment:* What can you do to add a little enjoyment to another's day? It can be as simple as telling a good joke. Jokes stimulate smiles and laughter and give people a lift for the rest of the day. I used to carry a bag of lollipops on airplanes for kids, flight attendants, or anybody who wanted to indulge a sweet tooth. I have friends who know how to perform simple magic tricks. Sometimes they do tricks just to bring a smile to the face of another person. Sometimes they do magic to help close six-figure sales. They know the power of adding a little good stuff, like enjoyment.

- *Enthusiasm:* Think of enthusiasm as a blend of positive

emotion and energy (this isn't a scientific or a dictionary definition). Enthusiasm makes ordinary events, processes, services, or interactions extraordinary.

- *Humor:* Laughter is good medicine for the soul. What product or service couldn't benefit from a spoonful of soul medicine? Even if your product or service is quite serious—and receiving your mail is, to most people, pretty serious business—you don't have to take yourself so seriously.

6. *Subtract "bad stuff."* What annoys or irritates you the most? Wouldn't it be great if others were vigilant enough to notice what those irritants are and, to the degree they could, reduce or eliminate them for you? That's what I mean by "subtract 'bad stuff'."

Of course one person's bad stuff isn't necessarily bad for another person. It's important to know that the stuff you're subtracting is better gone.

What constitutes bad stuff for most of us most of the time? Here is the worst of the bad stuff:

- *Waiting.* Who likes to wait? Not many. While waiting can help us develop patience, most of us get far more practice than we'd prefer. Don't you love prompt people? Don't you rejoice when your appointment starts and ends on time? Isn't it refreshing to see those who serve others move with a sense of urgency, a sense of respect for your time? Freds are good at minimizing or eliminating the waiting their customers and colleagues experience.

- *Defects*. It's true that nothing's perfect, that imperfection is the way of nature. But when we *pay* for something to be right or correct, it is maddening to experience a flaw. A simple furniture delivery can go from excitement over a new piece of furniture to stewing over the fact that the desk is scratched on one end because of a careless delivery person. Freds strive to make their work and services defect-free.

- *Mistakes*. If defects happen to things, mistakes happen to processes. What a drag when someone else makes a mistake, but you have to pay the consequences. ("I'm sorry, ma'am, but somebody in our office lost your application. I'll have to ask you to send it in again.") One of the most powerful things anybody can do to achieve Fred status is this: *Solve a problem you didn't create.* How's that again? Solve problems for people even if you weren't responsible for the mistake. ("I'm sorry, ma'am, but someone in processing lost your application. I'll be glad to take the information by phone to minimize the time you spend reapplying.") It's no compliment to be called a problem spotter, but the world loves problem solvers. Freds take responsibility for solving problems and mistakes even if they didn't initially create them.

- *Irritation and frustration.* Can you really eliminate those two negative emotions in another person? Indirectly, it is possible to start developing positive feelings in others. I'd been getting the runaround from the customer service department of an insurance company. I was so mad that I informed my principal contact that as soon as my policy expired, I wouldn't be doing business with his organization *ever again!* Evidently he didn't pass on the information. When my policy expired, a woman named Theresa called me about replacing the policy. I was incensed! "Doesn't the file say what a horrible, rotten experience I've had with your company?" I asked. "Do you have any idea how irritated and frustrated I've been when I've tried doing business with your company in the past?" Theresa paused for a moment, and then said, "I'm very sorry, Mr. Sanborn. I don't know what you've experienced in the past. But I promise you this: If you stay with us, I will personally service your account, and you won't be disappointed again." I did, and I wasn't. Freds work hard to minimize irritation and frustration for others and maximize positive feelings.

- *Misinformation.* Subtract as much of this stuff as you can. If you don't know the answer to a question, say so. And if there is a reason why you don't know, at least explain why that is and what you can offer in the way of accurate information. While nobody likes bad news, there is something worse: Good news that isn't exactly true. We get our hopes and expectations up when we gather information from others, and then our hopes are dashed on the rocks of reality. Freds get rid of misinformation. They are honest when they don't know the answer to a question and will do everything in their power to find the right answer.

7. *Simplify.* This is another superb "created" value. Make it easier for people to get what they need from you. Eliminate red tape and mind-numbing bureaucracy. Don't break any laws or do anything immoral, but think about the systems you are a part of. You know how things work. Where are the shortcuts? What does an insider—that would be you—know that would benefit an outsider?

If you want to be of greater service to others, use your knowledge and expertise to help them understand what appears to be a complex and overwhelming situation.

If you were to call the help desk of a computer manufacturer because you were totally perplexed trying to set up your new computer, wouldn't you want to talk to a Fred? A Fred would probably begin by saying, "I know how confusing this looks, but I'm going to help you get up and running quickly," and then he would proceed to simplify the situation. A non-Fred might range from being simply mechanical in his or her scripted responses to being downright condescending.

8. *Improve.* To improve means "to make better, to multiply

existing value." Do what you've always done, but do it better than you've ever done it. If you adopt that simple strategy, others will notice. In 1869 H. J. Heinz coined a phrase that describes the goal of every Fred: "To do the common thing uncommonly well."

Think of all the uncommon things you could do uncommonly well. Would an extra sentence or two in an e-mail make the difference between simply informative and truly helpful information? What kind of style can you bring to your phone manners? Are you able to transform a phone complainer into another committed customer, not just because you addressed the problem, but because of the way you addressed it?

Freds are always looking for ways, big and small, to improve the quality of their work and their interactions.

9. Surprise others. After hosting a large group of children and parents for our son Hunter's third birthday party, my wife and I were exhausted. We loaded up the Explorer, with Grandma on board too, and headed out for dinner. There was a lengthy wait at our first two restaurants of choice, so we ended up at a Perkins restaurant by default. This place epitomized "ordinary." The building was old, the interior needed an update, and the menu was basic. The only surprising thing was the service.

Our server was a young woman with a cheerful demeanor. While taking our order, she noticed the adults' slumping shoulders and heard Hunter complain of his hunger. She promised to bring our food right out.

In a few minutes she was back with a stuffed Curious George monkey under her arm. My son loves Curious George. "I just won this stuffed animal and really don't have much use for it," our server said. "I thought your son might enjoy it."

Hunter's face lit up as he accepted the unexpected gift. We thanked her and told her it was his birthday. "Well, happy birthday then!" she said and left to get our orders.

The food was pretty good, and the bill was typical. But the tip I left was exceptional, and our server deserved it (although I really don't think that was her ulterior motive). A thoughtful gesture from a nice person had totally surprised us and lifted our spirits.

10. Entertain others. "Gather 'round, one and all, watch and learn!" yelled the young man behind the marble table. "I am the King of Fudge!" For the next several minutes he narrated as he made a batch of fresh fudge, using a long paddle to mix and stir. The aroma was enticing and the demonstration informative. But it was the Fudge King's entertainment that held our attention.

If someone asked me to go watch fudge being made, let's face it, I'd pass. But our fudge master knew something about human behavior that all Freds know: People love to be entertained. We pay closer attention, learn faster, and are more engaged when we're entertained. I'm not talking about mindless entertainment. The King of Fudge had a reason for his performance: He wanted to sell more fudge. And he did.

GO WORK SOME MAGIC

All it takes to be an alchemist are the ordinary ingredients of the hours and minutes of each day. The worth of those minutes is determined by how you use them. Most people think creating value requires spending money, but Freds know that all it takes is a little imagination.

Apply the techniques and principles you've learned in this chapter. Then, like Fred, you'll become a present-day alchemist, changing the ordinary moments of your day into pure gold.

Seven

REINVENT YOURSELF REGULARLY

A sad employee left his job of many years
Most days he worked were like the day before
He wasn't disliked by colleagues, but he won't be missed
And while he made good money, he felt quite poor.

He always did what he was paid to do and nothing more
And he did without having any fun.
He performed his job the way he lived his life:
He did it the way it had always been done.

—MARK SANBORN

While not all change is good, staying the same can't be all good either. The only difference between a rut and a grave, as the old saying goes, is the depth.

Freds know that one of the most exciting things about life is that we awake each day with the ability to reinvent ourselves.

No matter what happened yesterday, today is a new day. While we can't deny the struggles and setbacks, neither should we be restrained by them.

You've never been a Fred, you say? You're talking ancient history! That was yesterday. Today you can begin the process of becoming who you want to be. If you hope to keep growing and going, all you need to do is seize the opportunity to reinvent yourself. You accomplish this by daily actions—big and small—that show your commitment to a new, improved version of yourself. Otherwise you'll fall behind in a competitive world.

Grow Yourself, Grow Your Value

The best way to grow your value is to grow yourself. Become a sponge for ideas. Take time to truly think about what you do and why you do it. So often we live our lives on autopilot, unable to distinguish between *activity* and *accomplishment*.

The more you grow as a person, the more you'll have to share with others. Think of personal growth as the modeling clay of your reinvention. The more clay you have, the larger and more detailed a sculpture you can create. The more you learn—not abstract knowledge, but practical education—the more raw material you will have to shape your personal work of art.

You increase in stature as you increase your mental, spiritual, and physical capabilities. As you grow you'll make new connections with people and ideas that will enable you to become a master craftsman of value.

BE LED BY COMPELLING REASONS

It won't help much to be driven to reinvent yourself and improve on your best. Being driven suggests an almost unhealthy compulsion to do something because you should, not because you want to. Acting out of obligation is a good way to short-circuit what being a Fred is all about.

My postal carrier, Fred, did an exceptional job because he enjoyed doing it. How could I tell? By the smile on his face and his whole demeanor. He just acted happy. He was having fun, not complying with some work mandate.

Having a goal to become more Fred-like in your work won't motivate you; having a compelling reason—a passion or purpose—to become more Fred-like is what will stir your motivation. Examples of compelling reasons might range from the positive effect you'll have on others to the joy of doing an extraordinary job to being a positive role model. Whatever reason or reasons you identify, let them draw the best out of you.

CAPITALIZE ON YOUR LIFE EXPERIENCES

In your life you've likely seen and experienced phenomenal things. And while you haven't exactly forgotten these things, you probably don't often bring them into your conscious awareness and use them productively.

If you want to reinvent yourself and improve for the future, spend some time reflecting on the past. What are the most important lessons you've learned? What did you once deeply desire to accomplish that you never attempted? Which people most shaped your life, and what did you learn from them? Whom do you admire the most? Which of their skills and characteristics would you like to develop in your life?

Buy a small journal. Jot down the answers to those questions. Also write down what you remember or learn each day. Capture and capitalize on the ideas that too often stay hidden in the rich storehouse of your mind.

Increase Your "IQ"

It isn't enough just to have good ideas if you don't do something with them.

Your ability to be a Fred depends on your IQ. Now don't be discouraged if you aren't in the Einstein brain category. By *IQ*, I mean "implementation quotient." In this case, IQ represents the difference between having a good idea and implementing it.

How many good ideas die for lack of action and follow-through on your part? Knowing you could have made someone's day and actually making his or her day are two dramatically different things.

One way to improve your IQ is to write down good ideas as they come to you, then put them on your daily to-do list. Sometimes inaction is the result of a poor memory, and what you commit to writing is easier to remember and act upon.

Share as a team _

IMPROVE ON THE BEST

Good ideas are all around you. Seek out what the best people are doing. Watch and learn. Then adapt and apply.

That last statement is the key. If you just copy what other capable people are doing, you'll only do as well as they do. The key is to adapt, to take good ideas from every source and then apply them with your own special flair.

You can learn from the other Freds of the world: people in other departments, in other organizations, in other industries, even in other countries. While the ideas you observe may not be an exact fit for you, with some tailoring you can go beyond simply duplicating to becoming truly innovative.

PRACTICE THE ONE-A-DAY PLAN

Good news: You don't have to do everything in an extraordinary manner. If you attempted that, you'd be bogged down before you ever left home in the morning.

Turning the ordinary into the extraordinary happens one act

at a time. So if you do just one extraordinary thing a day, whether at home or at work, seven days a week, fifty-two weeks a year (even while on vacation), your life will soon be a record book of the extraordinary.

One extraordinary act a day isn't overwhelming; it is very doable. Dozens of acts a day? Unrealistic. But one a day? Anyone can do that! Start by doing what you know you can do. As you continue reinventing yourself, supplement your one-a-day strategy by doing more. But build on that simple practice.

Think about it. All it takes is

- one thoughtful remark to a loved one each day to enrich a relationship;
- one exceptional performance a day to get the right kind of attention from your boss; or
- one unexpected act of service a day to turn the life of another in a positive direction.

Over time, the one-a-day principle will turn your mundane life into an extraordinary life—and it will do the same for others as well.

COMPETE...WITH YOURSELF!

It's common to compare ourselves with others. We want to know how we stack up compared to those around us. Are we better or worse, more skilled or less skilled, faster or slower? There's nothing inherently wrong with that, but it can drive you crazy. The reality is that there will always be people accomplishing more or less than you. The comparison game can be rigged simply by carefully choosing whom or what you measure yourself against.

It's a lot more productive—and fun—to compare and compete against yourself. The goal is ongoing improvement. Reinvention is positive change. Benchmark where you are against how far you've come and where you want to go.

Develop a baseline for your attempts to be like Fred. Keep track (don't keep score) of those ordinary things that you attempt to make extraordinary as well as the results they create. Continually look for ways to take your game to the next level.

THE RIPPLE EFFECT

I had just finished speaking to a group on the fifty-yard line of Atlanta's Georgia Dome. IBM, the host of this special event, had rented the facility. The participants, a group of one hundred highly creative Web designers, seemed to enjoy my speech.

After I had finished talking with a few audience members, a man near the field entrance approached me. He extended his hand and said, "I'm one of the bus drivers. They didn't really invite us to attend your presentation, but I stood in the back anyway. I like hearing speakers and learning new ideas. I want you to know that you really encouraged me. You see, I'm an inventor.

I've invented a new seat cushion people can use when attending events in stadiums just like this one. And I agreed with practically everything you said. Your words have encouraged me to keep trying."

The host company was very happy with my presentation that day. But the biggest reward came not from that or the fee I received, but from the feedback of an appreciative individual who wasn't even supposed to be in the audience.

Is it possible that you are making significant impressions on others and don't even know it? We need to be conscious not only of the primary effects of the things we do but of the secondary consequences, which are a ripple effect that touches far more people than those in our immediate presence.

You just never know who's watching and listening. Our lives, to paraphrase Shakespeare, play out on a stage.

Freds find satisfaction in their passion for significance. They distinguish themselves not by the results they've achieved, but by how they've affected and touched others.

Bob Briner, former president of ProServe and the author of several books, distinguished himself by living a life of service. His trademark was to ask clients, friends, and colleagues how he could serve them. It wasn't a hollow question; he really worked hard to serve others.

Just days before Bob succumbed to cancer, musician Michael W. Smith went to see him. Despite being weak and frail, Bob managed to ask his visitor one last question, "How can I serve you?"

Bob Briner was a Fred.

Whether they are formal leaders, entrepreneurs, employees, family members, or friends, Freds have a profound impact on others because of the example they set. Their efforts inspire, both directly and indirectly. That's one of the best reasons I know of for continually seeking to reinvent ourselves.

PART 3
DEVELOPING
OTHER FREDS

Within ten minutes of my house are two giant hardware stores that are known for their low prices. Each has an amazing selection, but the service you receive when you shop at these stores is ordinary. That's why I rarely go to either place.

Also ten minutes away is a smaller hardware store, probably one-quarter the size of its giant rivals. While the pricing is competitive at the smaller store, I never expect the prices to be the lowest.

But I don't mind—because every aisle is staffed with Freds.

I'm home-improvement challenged. I'm not so much in need of parts for the sprinkler system or washers for the plumbing as I'm in the market for solutions to domestic disasters.

When you walk into this smaller hardware store, highly knowledgeable and helpful staff are near the door. If they don't have the answer to your questions, they know the man or woman who does. They don't tell you where to find the widgets and thingamajigs; they take you to the exact spot where the stuff is. And they usually ask enough questions to find out if what you're planning to buy is what you really need.

This retailer is an example of what happens when you populate an organization with Fred-like employees.

Maybe that's one of the best-kept secrets of competing successfully: having Fred-like employees at every level in your organization.

So how do you get them? In an age of high employee

turnover and nosediving customer loyalty, developing Freds should be a critical priority for every business. Having Freds as teammates and leaders within your organization will distinguish it as a truly extraordinary company.

All organizations have access to the same information, consultants, training, compensation systems, perks, and benefits. So why do some soar while others flop? The difference is not in the things—processes, functions, and structures—but in the people. Uninspired people rarely do inspired work.

Passionate people in an organization are different. They do ordinary things extraordinarily well. Even if some of their ideas are average, they still are useful.

Customers don't have relationships with organizations; they form relationships with individuals. Passionate employees, whether they are salespeople, technicians, or service reps, constantly show their commitment to customers. They do this by demonstrating their passion about what they do. As a result, Freds accomplish more than their blasé colleagues and are better able to meet the challenges of limited resources.

Not surprisingly, Freds are also generally happier because people doing good work feel good, and people doing exceptional work feel, well, *exceptional*. Accomplishment contributes greatly to satisfaction.

How can you develop Freds? The next four chapters spell it out:

F—Find

R—Reward

E—Educate

D—Demonstrate

Simple? Yes. Easy? No.

But whoever said it would be easy to be extraordinary—or to find and develop extraordinary people?

Eight

FIND

> There is something that is much more scarce, some-
> thing finer by far, something rarer than ability. It is
> the ability to recognize ability.
>
> —ELBERT HUBBARD

Are Freds born or made?

Certainly, some people are born with a predisposition to be Fred-like. Others may not start out with that orientation, but in time they learn how to be that way. Still others may leverage their natural disposition with a deliberate effort to be even more Fredlike.

In any case, the more Freds you attract to your organization or team, the more successful you'll be. Before I explain how to help people be more Fred-like, let's look at some ways to find the Freds who are already out there.

There are three basic ways to seek out Freds, both inside and outside your organization.

1. Let Them Find You

Is your organization a Fred-magnet? If you really want your company to be world-class, it must become the kind of place that attracts Freds.

According to Dale Dauten, author of *The Gifted Boss,* people want to work in organizations and for bosses who offer them a change and a chance. The change is the opportunity to work for an organization that recognizes, rewards, encourages, and values Freds. The chance is to become better than one has ever been.

These are the factors most Freds want and seek.

But here's the catch: If you don't already have some living, breathing Freds doing exceptional things for your customers or clients, your place of business or organization isn't going to be perceived as the hot place to work. If your employees and colleagues don't go home at the end of the day and rave to family and friends about what a great company they work for, don't count on word of mouth to bring you a landslide of Fred-like applicants.

Sometimes you can acquire exceptional people from other departments in your own organization. They may be feeling restrained by their current boss or situation and are looking for a place to "grow and show"—to develop their abilities and demonstrate what they're capable of doing.

Make your area a Fred oasis. Really good department heads

have often told me that they got their best team players from other departments where they weren't taken good care of.

2. Discover Dormant Freds

Finding Freds is often no more difficult than uncovering the latent talent of those you already work with.

Remember when downsizing was so prevalent? Certainly some of it was necessary, but I've always felt much of it was a "quick fix." Managers believed it was easier to let employees go than to release their talents and abilities. What would have happened if managers had taken the time to uncover the hidden contributions employees could have made to justify their place in the organization?

Many employees are "loaded" for making the ordinary extraordinary, but nobody has figured out how, figuratively speaking, to "pull the trigger."

Discovering talent is often nothing more than uncovering it. When you trust your people with time—the most valuable asset—to reveal their talents, you'll see just how many Freds there are in your organization.

Are there any tricks or techniques for spotting potential Freds? In theory at least, everyone has the potential to make the ordinary extraordinary. But the kind of person I am referring to here is already inclined to do so. The most practical suggestion I can give you is to pay attention. Watch for people who do things with flair (not to be confused with showing off or trying to attract attention). An exceptionally well-done project, an elegant client meeting, or a clever suggestion are all possible tip-offs that a dormant Fred is standing right before your eyes.

3. Hire Freds

When you have exhausted the potential "Fred pool" in your own backyard, then you need to know how to identify a potential Fred in an interview. Here's what you should ask a prospective Fred:

- Who are your heroes? Why?
- Why would anyone do more than necessary?
- Tell me three things that you think would delight most customers/clients/consumers.
- What's the coolest thing that's happened to you as a customer?
- What is service?

Here are some questions to ask yourself about a potential Fred:

- What do I remember most about this person?
- What's the most extraordinary thing he or she has ever done?
- How badly would this person be missed if he or she left his or her current position?

BUILD YOUR FRED TEAM

What would you consider best: (a) an ordinary team led by a Fred or (b) a team of Freds led by an ordinary leader?

Okay, it was a trick question! The answer, for me at least, is "none of the above." I want a team of Freds led by a Fred. Only when leaders and followers share the same values and commitment can any organization truly maximize the potential of the Fred Factor.

There are lots of people like Fred out there in the marketplace. The challenge is finding them. The solution is to discover them, attract them, and hire them. All three involve slightly different strategies, but each complements the others. Over time you can build a winning team of Freds.

★ Nine ★

REWARD

> No man can become rich without himself enriching others.
>
> —ANDREW CARNEGIE

Dr. Michael LeBoeuf, in his insightful book *The Greatest Management Principle in the World,* sums it up quite neatly when he tells us we don't get the behavior we hope for, beg for, or demand. We get the behavior we reward.

Dr. LeBoeuf also explains more fully that it is a matter of rewarding the right behavior and using the right rewards.

Following are some examples of how this works.

THE ATLANTA BUSBOY

This instructive and touching story was related to me by Jim Cathcart, author of *The Acorn Principle* and CEO of the Cathcart Institute, Inc.

A few years ago I was traveling through the airport in Atlanta, Georgia. At the food court between concourses, I stopped for a breakfast snack only to be confronted by thousands of fellow travelers also stopping to eat there. The place was packed! Every table had people standing nearby waiting to take over seats on a moment's notice.

As I stood sipping my coffee and eating a muffin, I noticed a busboy cleaning the tables. He was sadly slumped over and looked defeated and depressed. He dragged himself slowly from table to table, clearing the trash and wiping the tabletops. He made eye contact with no one, and just watching him, I started becoming depressed!

I caught myself mid-emotion and said to myself, "Somebody has to do something about this." So I did. I disposed of my trash and walked over to the busboy. I tapped him on the shoulder (which made him recoil as if he had been caught in a crime).

"What you are doing here sure is important," I said.

"Huh?" he replied.

I repeated myself and added, "If you weren't doing what you are doing, it wouldn't be five minutes before there was trash everywhere, and people would stop coming in here. What you are doing is important, and I just wanted to say thanks for doing it." Then I walked away.

He was in shock. (Perhaps no one had ever spoken to

him that way before.) When I had walked about ten feet, I turned and looked back at him. In the time it had taken me to travel just that distance, I swear he had grown six inches! He was standing straighter, almost smiling, and even looking some people in the eye. Now he had not become "Service Man," spreading cheer and goodwill. He was merely working a bit more effectively and no longer looking depressed.

What I had done in the overall scheme of things was trivial. My comments did not change the world…or did they? By simply pointing out how the busboy's behavior affected other people, I had added dignity to his work. My simple acknowledgment of his worth had raised his opinion of himself in that role.

I love Jim's story (who by the way was quite a Fred himself in this incident) because it illustrates a key principle: *When you don't see much meaning in what you do, you won't bring much value to what you do.*

Jim helped that busboy see the bigger picture of his importance. And that wasn't all. In the course of that workday, the busboy probably came into contact with hundreds of people, all of whom were traveling somewhere to interact with still more people. No doubt some of the busboy's heightened sense of self-worth "infected" the people around him, and those good vibes radiated to others in distant locations. That's what happens when the Fred Factor is fully operative: Even the smallest gestures make the world a better place.

Intention Counts Too

It's just as important to reward a Fred for good intentions as for stellar outcomes. While no one likes to fail, it is much more important for an employee to know that taking chances to do the right thing will be acknowledged, not punished. Nobody hits a home run every time. (In fact, home-run hitters tend to strike out more than other batters.) When people feel that their contributions are unappreciated, they will stop trying. And when that happens, innovation dies.

Implement Your Reward Strategy

Take a good look around your organization or the areas where you have influence. Rewarding others is not that hard to do. This is all you have to do on a consistent basis:

- Make sure all of your team members know that they are making an important contribution or have the ability to do so.
- Tell your team members what kind of difference they are making. Be specific. Cite increased production, sales, and

hires; commendations from outside sources; insightful suggestions; increased motivation and enthusiasm—anything
and everything that applies.

- Be sure that positive feedback about their efforts is a rule,
not an exception.

- Create an award. Consider a trophy or a plaque or even a
small amount of cash. Don't make the value of the award
so large in monetary terms that it looks like a Fred bribe.
Have fun sharing tangible recognition. Consider giving
multiple Fred awards each month if several people are
deserving.

- Get the leader (CEO, president, director) of your organization to personally recognize the Freds. Ask him or her to
send a note or to make a phone call letting the employee
know the contribution has been noticed and appreciated.

Remember the reward formula and apply it often: Recognize
a contribution, reinforce its positive effects on your business, and
repeat. And don't forget that sincere praise for trying—written as
well as spoken frequently in public and in private—is one of the
best rewards.

Ten

EDUCATE

> The brighter you are, the more you have to learn.
>
> —DON HEROLD

When you consider the education and training employees or others under your direction receive in your organization, what is being taught and how well is it being taught?

If people are taught only ordinary subjects and skills, they'll only know how to be *ordinary*. Every organization in the world today should be teaching employees how to be *extraordinary*.

In general, managers and leaders universally embrace the concepts I've used throughout this book, or at least they *say* they do. Curiously, though, I rarely see managers or organizations attempting to teach the principles embodied in *The Fred Factor*.

Part of the Fred Factor philosophy is having fun. That's what makes work interesting and exciting not only for the people doing the work but for customers and coworkers as well.

In the spirit of fun, you could call this chapter "Providing a Freducation." Of course, it would ruin the FRED acronym I'm using in this section, but what I'm really suggesting is consciously teaching people ways to think and perform like a Fred.

An unexpected benefit of teaching these things is that it will make you a better manager or leader, not to mention a better person. You'll increase your Freducation—your skill set—in the process. Here's how to do it.

1. FIND EXAMPLES EVERYWHERE

What do you notice when you're on vacation? If you're a photographer, you probably have a greater awareness of photo opportunities. If you're a musician, you most likely pay closer attention to the music being played or performed at the location. My point: Your interests focus your awareness.

As you become increasingly interested in developing the art of the extraordinary in yourself and others, you'll notice more and more examples. Not only will you see little things done in exceptional ways and notice the people who make the extra effort to be extraordinary, but you'll also notice "anti-Fred" examples as well. You'll find yourself thinking, *There's a great example of what not to do!*

Record in writing all ideas and examples. If you run across them in your reading, highlight them. Clip out newspaper articles. Put all these examples in a Fred file, and soon you'll have some of the best training illustrations imaginable because they're not abstract or contrived. Nothing inspires people more than an example directly experienced or indirectly learned from a real-life incident.

Challenge the people on your team to collect examples as well. Begin or end meetings with the question, "Who's got a Fred example to share?" Make it a friendly contest with a nominal award. Maybe even post the "Fred of the Week" where others can see it as well.

2. Dissect and Debrief

Generally, a positive change will not endure unless we understand why it worked. Even the best examples can lose impact if we don't take time to consider exactly what happened.

Dissecting and debriefing is a way of accomplishing four things: (1) identifying the specific good idea behind the example, (2) adapting the idea to your situation, (3) looking for ways to improve it, and (4) identifying opportunities to apply it.

The process looks like this:

- *The good idea.* How did that make you feel? What makes that example cool? What makes it an example of what *not* to do? What's the basic idea here?

- *Adapting the idea to your situation.* Would that work for you? How could it work for you? What would you have to do, or do differently, to benefit from this example?

- *Looking for ways to improve it.* What would make this idea even better? What would you do differently? What would make our customers or clients appreciate this even more?
- *Opportunities for application.* When could you use this idea? Where? With whom? When will you start?

3. TEACH MIRACLE WORKING

My friend and fellow speaker Don Hutson has an important insight about "miracle" actions or responses that individuals and organizations are able to pull off for others. He asks, "When do these miracles usually happen?" The answer: When there's a crisis. It's true that there's nothing like a crisis to get our attention and make us perform beyond our present capabilities.

But that's not the critical point. Don's message is more important: Don't wait for a crisis! Perform miracles on a regular basis. Don correctly concludes that most of these "miracles" are performed by an individual with a big heart and a caring spirit, which, interestingly, is an accurate description of the kind of person who understands the Fred Factor.

Do you expect miracle working on a regular basis? Or do you reserve such extraordinary performance for a crisis? Teach the Fred Factor as a form of daily miracle working. (The size of the miracle is less important than its frequency.)

4. Pull, Don't Push

You can't command someone to be a Fred. You can't require some-one to practice the Fred Factor. You can try, of course. But it won't work. Command-and-control short-circuits the spirit of the Fred Factor, which is about opportunity, not obligation.

Here's what you can do: Invite people to join you. In other words, pull, don't push. Use your enthusiasm and commitment to gain their participation and involvement. The most powerful tool you have for spreading the Fred Factor throughout your organiza-tion is your own behavior—the example of your life and the effect it has on others.

The best Freducators are themselves Freds. They bring these principles and practices to bear on how they teach, train, and de-velop others. After all, as John Maxwell says, "You teach what you know, but you reproduce who you are."

Eleven

DEMONSTRATE

> You can preach a better sermon with your life than
> with your lips.
>
> —OLIVER GOLDSMITH

Do you have a friend or acquaintance who inspires you by his or her example?

I have a friend who lives in a city where my wife and I often visit relatives. He is the epitome of the southern gentleman. A highly successful businessman with exceptional taste, he owns and pilots his own airplane, and his home and furnishings are impressive. Yet despite the outer trappings of success, he is a most humble and sincere human being.

Whenever I'm in his town, I make it a point to have lunch with him. Whenever he hears that I am coming, he always asks me, "Is there anything I can do for you while you're here?"

Isn't that the essential question the Freds of the world ask, either aloud or silently, of the people they know and serve?

Some might ask that question superficially, but I know from

my friend's character and behavior that he is completely serious. If I said I needed a car to get around, I know with certainty he'd lend me one of his—or find one I could borrow. That's the kind of person he is.

But my friend does more than offer to extend himself to make my visit more enjoyable. He inspires me to act similarly, to strive to be the kind of person he is. While he has never coached or counseled me on how to be of greater service or how to be what I've called more Fred-like, he has done more than anyone else I've met to instill that desire within me.

He inspires me with the example of his life.

The Magic Question

What could you do to set an example and inspire your employees to serve your customers, vendors, and fellow employees better?

Here are four simple suggestions:

1. Inspire, but don't intimidate. When I share the story of Fred the Postman with audiences, the reaction I like best goes something like this: "Cool! I could do that too!"

If Fred came across as superhuman or inherently extraordinary, he wouldn't inspire people; he'd intimidate them. Fred inspires people like you and me because he's an ordinary guy doing an extraordinary job.

Your example should be down-to-earth and doable. If you

come across as genetically engineered for exceptional performance, others who feel they lack that special DNA will opt out of even trying.

2. Involve. Here's a radical idea for you to consider: *Team Fred.* There's no rule that says a team can't harness and benefit from the Fred Factor.

Many years ago a buddy of mine found out about a family that couldn't afford a good Thanksgiving dinner, so he purchased all the fixings and delivered them to their home the day before the holiday.

The next Thanksgiving he invited me to join him in doing something nice for people. It was a neat thing to do, and I've since invited others to join me in similar activities.

That's the power of involvement. It's far more effective than suggesting or asking.

What can you do to involve others in purposeful acts of "Fredness"?

3. Initiate. Don't wait for "the right moment." It will never come. Don't wait until somebody else goes first. Maybe someone will, but it's unlikely. Don't wait for the perfect opportunity. Just take an opportunity and make it as perfect as you can.

You can set the pace for extraordinary performance in your organization, but only if you initiate. That means taking action. Boldly. Quickly.

Be humble in your motives, but not in your example. Don't

act like a Fred for the recognition; do it to create participation. You are the spark that sets others on fire when you initiate.

4. Improvise. If I were to give you a homework assignment that would best teach the Fred Factor, it might be to attend an "improv" comedy performance. The beauty of improv is that it proves you can make just about any circumstance or situation funny. As in life, the situation doesn't determine the outcome; the participants do.

Take what life gives you. You might become a positive example not because of your situation, but in spite of it!

You may have the most dead-end job on the planet, but that shouldn't keep you from reinventing yourself and your job. In the process of improvising—trying stuff to see what works—you'll probably improve your job (or relationship or situation). And, hey, even if you don't, at least you won't be bored!

Forget that foolish saying, Those who can, do; and those who can't, teach. Not only is this statement derogatory and insulting to the dedicated professionals in education and training, but with a few exceptions, it just ain't so.

The reality? Those who do best teach best. The man or woman who can demonstrate a lesson with his or her life most powerfully impacts others.

When those who know are able to show, those who learn are able to grow. That's what a good Freducation is all about.

Go Spread Fred

Now that I trust you are convinced you want to be a Fred yourself, here are three other ways to help make this a world full of Freds:

1. Recognize the Freds in your life. Reflect back on your life. Who have been the Freds—the relatives, teachers, pastors, rabbis, friends, and others—who have made the biggest difference in your life? Maybe it was somebody you encountered in your business yesterday. Whoever and whenever, don't take lightly the extraordinary things people have done and do for you.

2. Acknowledge Freds for their contribution. Once you realize who the Freds in your life have been, make time to let them know how much you have appreciated their efforts. Write each of them a letter or a note. Send them gifts. Write articles or letters to the editor—and make sure your Freds get copies. Nominate them for Fred Awards (see www.fredfactor.com for details). Make sure they know they are valued and appreciated.

3. Pay Freds back. The only thing better than an acknowledgment is action. Choose to do something extraordinary, and dedicate it to someone who inspired you. The best payback, as the popular book and movie by the same name say, is to "pay it forward."

Fred the Postman has already started a chain reaction, beginning in my life and in the lives of his customers. He has affected hundreds, if not thousands, as I've shared his story. But think of the people who must have had a positive impact on him! The chain reaction began long before Fred started delivering mail on my street.

Using the Fred Factor won't cure the common cold or bring about world peace, but it will warm the lives of many and create peace in your corner of the world.

Isn't it great knowing you have the ability to show others how to make the ordinary extraordinary?

PART 4

FOR THE LOVE OF FRED

Twelve

FRED TODAY

> We are what we repeatedly do. Excellence, then, is
> not an act, but a habit.
>
> —ARISTOTLE

I'm frequently asked about Fred. Where is he today? What is he doing?

As of this writing Fred is doing his typical exceptional job of delivering mail in Denver.

Recently, the U.S. Postal Service recognized Fred for his years of service with a special ceremony at his station. I had the privilege of speaking to Fred's coworkers.

Fred was there with his wife, Kathie, and other family members. His coworkers were extremely proud of Fred and the honor he was receiving. After so many years of telling audiences about Fred, I was gratified to see him finally receiving from his employer the formal recognition he so richly deserved, recognition that Fred's customers have lavished on him over the years.

A local Denver television station was there to cover the event, and later there was a special piece about Fred on the evening news. The camera showed him delivering mail on his route, and the story included brief interviews with his "customers" who uniformly expressed their admiration and appreciation.

Because of the television show, viewers learned that I was the speaker telling the Fred Factor story and writing the book. As a result, I've received phone calls and e-mails about Fred. The most common theme: I know Fred too, and you're right; he's amazing!

A woman on Fred's route called to relate this story: She had lived in Washington Park for many years as a single mom. She raised her daughter alone, and Fred delivered their mail throughout the years her daughter was growing up.

The woman's mother was in town visiting, and as sometimes happens, Grandmother was vocal in her disagreement with the parenting techniques the mom had used with the now full-grown granddaughter. It bothered the woman, and when Fred walked onto the porch that day to deliver her mail, she felt comfortable enough with him to do a little venting.

When Fred heard the story, he was adamant: "I've watched you raise your daughter from a little girl to a grown woman, and you've been a wonderful mother! She's turned out great, and you have nothing to feel bad about. You should be proud of the job you've done."

Those kind words made all the difference in her day. All she needed to go from feeling awful to feeling awesome was a little encouragement from someone she knew and trusted. That some-one was her postal carrier, Fred.

To Fred this woman was not just a customer. Over time he had built a friendship that made the single mom feel comfortable confiding in him. When a time of personal need came, Fred was ready and able to provide the perspective she needed.

I've also learned more about Fred's background. He started playing music when he was eight years old and as a young man became a drummer for a band. He met Kathie one night at a performance.

Because of his interest in music, one of Fred's hobbies is refin-ishing drums and donating them to school music departments. Once, he received a call from the band teacher at a nearby school who was losing drummers at an alarming rate. Fred diagnosed the problem: With only snare drums to play, the drummers were get-ting bored.

That's what motivated Fred to start refurbishing drums. He would spend two hours a night, three days a week at the school, working with the kids and providing them drum sets to play. But what else would you expect from Fred?

Why Is Fred a "Fred"?

Now that you know what Fred does and how he does it, you need to know why.

In all the years I had known Fred, I had never asked him what may be the most important question: "Why do you do what you do?" His extraordinary work as a postal carrier wasn't making him rich or famous.

So I put the question to Fred. His answers were concise but carefully considered. Fred is one of those people who is very purposeful about how he lives his life. He understands himself and what motivates him. Here is a summary of what Fred told me motivates him to be a "Fred":

1. *Do good and you'll feel good.* "I have to feel good about myself each day, and the satisfaction of taking care of people helps me do that," Fred said.

Fred finds being of service to others gratifying. He has uncovered a secret: When you do good, you feel good. Pursuing good feelings as a means to an end doesn't work. As philosophers and theologians have known for centuries, being of service to others isn't just the right thing to do, it's the gratifying thing to do.

2. *The best never rest.* Fred continued to answer my question by saying, "I'm my own worst critic. I've been told that I am a perfectionist. But I have a tremendous need to accomplish as much as I can each day. I take care of people who don't always know what I've done for them. But even if nobody else knows, I do. So my personal commitment is to do the best I can. And you know what? It doesn't take much extra time or effort to do what I do."

Fred is an example of noble effort combined with heart. If Fred were just a perfectionist, he wouldn't have the same effect on people. But Fred cares as much for the people he serves as he does for how well he does his job. That makes all the positive difference in the world.

3. Treat customers and others as friends. Nobody can argue that Fred provides world-class service. Ironically, he is able to do that because he doesn't think in terms of "customer service."

"I want to go home at the end of the day feeling like I've taken care of my folks," Fred said. "I don't think of them as postal customers, but as friends who appreciate me for helping make their lives a little easier."

In the course of delivering mail, Fred moves advertisements that are stuck in doors and newspapers scattered on sidewalks. He even moves recycling boxes out of sight into less noticeable places. The postal customers' homes look neater, and burglars and mischief makers have one less clue that no one is home.

"I guess you could say I'm my own Neighborhood Watch program," Fred chuckles.

4. The impact you have on others is the reward. You might think that Fred would expect or at least hope for the recognition he's received. But that's not Fred. When it comes to this book and any attention he has received, Fred says, "I'm overwhelmed."

He never sought recognition or accolades. He did what he did and continues to do what he does for the simple reason that he feels it is the right thing to do. You and I aren't surprised that his exceptional service has brought him great attention, but Fred is.

The rewards and recognition are nothing more than icing on the cake for him. The cake is doing his best work and being of service.

"It doesn't take much time to make somebody smile. And if I am able to make someone on my route smile, that's my reward," says Fred.

5. *Live the golden rule.* Fred notices that his approach to life isn't the norm today. "I see a lot of 'me, me, me' in our culture. I choose to give people a few less things to worry about. For me it is as simple as living the golden rule—treating others as I'd like to be treated."

6. *Fear nothing except to waste the moment.* I asked Fred, "What one final piece of advice would you like to give readers of this book?"

He didn't hesitate. "Look to every day as a new day, and make each day better than the last. Even on my days off, I have goals, and I feel like I need to get a lot done. If I feel like I wasted the day, I don't sleep quite as well at night."

That is Fred's modus operandi. He doesn't do what he does to increase market share, win awards, or grow earnings. He practices the art of the extraordinary because of his personal commitment to make the most of each day.

Thirteen

THE FRED SPIRIT

At the Day of Judgment we shall not be asked what
we have read but what we have done.

—THOMAS À KEMPIS

The Fred Factor is based on an extraordinary postal carrier. Think of it as Fred's story.

Of course, the spirit he exemplifies has been present in men, women, and children throughout history. Some have achieved public acclaim and have been noted in history. Others are lost to history because they quietly did their work in relative obscurity.

Whom do we most remember? We remember those who lived to serve others. We are most impressed and affected not by what people gain but by what they give; not by what they conquer but by what they contribute. And we recognize in every Fred a common purpose modeled after a generosity of spirit that has been among us since the beginning of time.

Having the Heart of a Fred

It was the first day of pre-kindergarten, and I was walking with my son Hunter into the school building. As we approached, he asked, "Dad, what's the most important thing of all?" I was impressed that my then five-year-old was insightful enough to ask for advice about how to do well in school. I thought for a moment and started to answer with some ideas about obeying the teachers, learning as much as you can, and playing well with the other kids. Before I could finish, Hunter interrupted.

"D-a-a-a-a-d," he strung the word out with a hint of exasperation. "The most important thing of all is love."

His answer stopped me in my tracks. Dad hadn't quite gotten it. Hunter was asking for simple advice, but he was thinking profound thoughts.

If you were to ask me what the most important thing about the Fred Factor is, I'd have to answer the same way. *The most important thing is love of others.* Not necessarily a sugary, let's-all-sing-"We-Are-the-World" kind of love, but a stable, meaningful generosity of spirit that enables us to do things for others—those we know and those we don't—because at base level we choose to give of ourselves.

I've learned that such generosity of spirit reveals itself, among other things, through action. I can love someone I don't necessarily like. I can do something or act toward that person in a certain way because I know it is the right thing to do even if I don't feel warm and fuzzy doing it.

So here's my working definition of generosity of spirit: It is the commitment to treat a person with dignity and kindness regardless of how you feel about him or her.

It is much easier to act with generosity toward lovable people. Just about anybody can do that. But to do that with people of poor behavior or negative circumstance is the tough challenge of life.

Mother Teresa took care of the lepers and the poor and the downcast of the world, and we consider her a saint.

Marva Collins sticks in my mind as a woman who truly cared about her students. Years ago she started a program in Chicago called Westside Prep and vowed that she would not let her students fail. I'm sure some of those students frustrated or angered her. But she helped them anyway.

The more you care about others—do those things that treat them with dignity, that serve and enrich their lives—the easier it is to like them. People become more lovable when they are loved.

Most of this book has been about the *what* and the *how* of the Fred Factor, but if you don't understand the *why*, you'll soon tire of the journey. It is the *why* behind the Fred Factor that will sustain and guide you.

Fred the Postman genuinely cares about people. He cares deeply about his customers and coworkers. And it shows. He does his ordinary job each day with compassion and heart, and his work becomes extraordinary.

This book is a short history of a particular Fred, the one who delivered my mail and became my friend. But there have been many Freds in history.

What makes any act extraordinary is doing it with heart. What makes any life extraordinary is living it with love.

That's the secret of the Fred Factor.

Appendix

THE FRED REPORT CARD

Measure what you treasure.

Would you like a way to evaluate your efforts toward becoming a Fred? I've created a report card you can use to both assess your efforts and remind you of the key elements of being a Fred. Use it as a positive reminder to keep you focused on the process.

I. AWARENESS

Ignorance isn't bliss, it's blind. A lack of awareness prevents us from consciously focusing on what's important. Awareness colors our perspective. Those values you keep foremost in your mind become the values you are most likely to live out.

In this case, awareness is about holding the example of Fred as a role model for your own behavior. It means being completely familiar with the four principles presented in chapter 2: Everyone Makes a Difference; Success Is Built on Relationships; You Must Continually Create Value for Others, and It Doesn't Have to Cost a Penny; and You Can Reinvent Yourself Regularly.

2. Agenda

Your agenda is your plan. It marks your determination to do those things you believe to be important. You can know something and do nothing about it. An agenda moves you from awareness to intention.

Look at your daily to-do list. Does it include the kinds of tasks that will add value to your work? Build better relationships? Make a positive difference in the world?

Your agenda answers the question, What are you planning to do to become a Fred?

3. Attitude

Here's an interesting dilemma: You can do all the right things, but if they're done for the wrong reasons or with the wrong attitude, your efforts will be short-circuited.

What won't work: acting like Fred because you feel you have to. *What will work:* acting like Fred because you want to.

Attitude colors everything you and I do in life.

A positive attitude allows you to see the things you undertake as an opportunity, not an obligation.

A positive attitude looks for the best, not the worst, in circumstances.

A positive attitude is "can-do," not "must-do."

A positive attitude is hopeful, not pessimistic.

And if you want to see the effects, reread chapter 1: "The First Fred."

4. ACTION

Intention without action is only a dream. In the end it isn't what we want to do or plan to do but what we actually do that makes any difference.

How far apart are your intentions to be like Fred and the actions you consistently take each day?

5. ACCOMPLISHMENT

You might think action is the last category on the report card, but it's not. The final way to score yourself is by evaluating what you accomplish.

Why is it that some people do the same or similar things others do but accomplish significantly more? Often there are subtle differences in the things they do, in the actions they take.

Evaluating accomplishment gives you a way to fine-tune your efforts for maximum impact.

Are you achieving the accomplishments you hoped for? Are the time and energy you are investing to be a Fred paying off for others? For yourself?

If you score less than an A in accomplishment, go back to your awareness, agenda, attitude, and action to diagnose opportunities for improvement.

Of course the good news is that your efforts will sometimes make a tremendous positive difference to others, though you may never find out about it. So don't be too tough on yourself. The fact that you are trying and doing your best is undoubtedly adding to the lives of others.

Team Fred Report Card

- Does each person on your team know that he or she makes a difference?
- Does everyone know how to build relationships?
- Does everyone know how to create value?
- Do team members realize how much more they could reinvent themselves and their business through innovation and passionate commitment?

ABOUT THE AUTHOR

MARK SANBORN is an international best-selling author and one of the youngest members ever inducted into the Speaker Hall of Fame. He is the president of Sanborn and Associates, Inc., an idea studio for leadership. Mark has spoken on leadership, change, teamwork, customer service, and motivation in every state in the United States as well as in eleven countries. He has served as the president of the National Speakers Association, an association of experts who speak professionally.

For more than thirty years, Mark has devoted himself to researching and studying leadership and applying what he has learned as a practitioner. His client list includes Fortune 500 companies, universities, associations, and churches.

Mark has also written and edited several books, including:

Teambuilt: Making Teamwork Work

Upgrade! Proven Strategies for Dramatically Increasing Personal and Professional Success

Sanborn on Success

Meditations for the Road Warrior (editor)

Best Practices in Customer Service (contributor)

For more information about Mark and the services he offers, visit www.marksanborn.com or call 800-650-3343.

Also available from Random House

NATURAL BORN WINNERS

Robin Sieger

Everyone is born with the potential to be a winner. So why are some people successful and others not? Why are some people happy and optimistic and others miserable? It's not down to luck: the answer lies in principles of mental conditioning, attitude and self-belief. These principles can be taught and followed.

Robin Sieger was inspired to create the **Natural Born Winners** programme following his experience of cancer at just thirty years of age. His research has involved success-oriented individuals from the British Army's elite Special Air Service Regiment, to professors of Strategic Management, and successful entrepreneurs. He uses facts, stories and humour to show the reader how to think like a champion, act like a champion, and be a Natural Born Winner.

£9.99
ISBN 0099476673

SUPERCOACHING

Ben Renshaw & Graham Alexander

How to use coaching to improve your work and personal life

SuperCoaching is for anyone wanting to succeed in a frenetic and unpredictable world.

We no longer have the time and cannot afford the effort to just get the job done in the traditional ways. We must now put relationships at the top of our agenda and deliver on what we know is true – that our colleagues, customers, friends and family are our greatest asset.

SuperCoaching shows you how to follow coaching principles that have made coaching the most powerful personal and professional development approach and fastest growing profession in the world today.

Filled with expert advice and practical suggestions, it gives the reader the necessary skills and confidence to implement the ideas put forward and to benefit from the extraordinary results that coaching offers.

£8.99
ISBN 1844137015

LUCKY OR SMART

Bo Peabody

Learn how to make your own luck

In November 1995, Bo Peabody, a 23-year-old university graduate, convinced New Enterprise Associates to invest $3 million in Tripod, an internet company enabling anyone with access to the internet to build their own web page.

By the middle of 1997, Tripod had attracted one million registered members. The company never posted a profit and generated barely any revenue.

On December 30th 1997, Bo Peabody was offered $58 million for Tripod. The payment came in the form of stocks in Lycos, another internet start-up, and over two years Bo watched his $58 million increase ten-fold.

By December 31st 1999, just before the bubble burst, Bo had sold every share of his Lycos stock.

Over the last 4 years, many people have asked Bo: 'Were you lucky or smart?' His response is always: 'I was smart enough to realise I was getting lucky.'

Read his story and learn how to make your own luck...

£7.99
ISBN 1844136914